2

OUTLINE STUDIES OF THE
TABERNACLE

ADA R. HABERSHON

kregel
PUBLICATIONS

Grand Rapids, MI 49501

NOTE TO THE READER

Because of the unfamiliarity of most of us today with the Roman numeral system, used throughout this book for chapter numbers, the following conversion table may offer welcome assistance to many readers:

i 1	xxii 22
ii 2	xxiii 23
iii 3	xxiv 24
iv 4	xxv 25
v 5	xxvi 26
vi 6	xxvii 27
vii 7	xxviii 28
viii 8	xxix 29
ix 9	xxx 30
x 10	xl 40
xi 11	l 50
xii 12	lx 60
xiii 13	lxx 70
xiv 14	lxxx 80
xv 15	xc 90
xvi 16	c 100
xvii 17	cx 110
xviii 18	cxx 120
xvix 19	cxxx 130
xx 20	cxl 140
xxi 21	cl 150

Outline Studies of the Tabernacle, illustrated edition by Ada R. Habershon. © 1974 by Kregel Publications, a division of Kregel, Inc., P. O. Box 2607, Grand Rapids, MI 49501. Published under special arrangements with Pickering & Inglis, Glasgow, Scotland. All rights reserved. First Kregel Publications edition: 1974.

Cover illustration and design: Don Ellens

Library of Congress Cataloging Card No. 73-85298

ISBN   0-8254-2820-3 (pbk.)

8 9 printing / year 05

Printed in the United States of America

Preface

" JESUS Himself drew near, and went with them. . . . And beginning at Moses, and all the prophets, He expounded unto them in all the Scriptures the things concerning Himself." " Things concerning Himself," would be a truthful title for this little book, which, at the eve of its going to press, my dear friend, its gifted and instructed writer, has asked me to preface—a request to which I gladly accede, though feeling unable to write but a few broken words.

The subject is one that has lain as a burning coal on my heart for now "these forty years," influencing my ministry in the Gospel beyond saying. To-day I feel more deeply than ever its unspeakable import, containing as it does, both in its history and mystery, the basis of all that is fundamental in the great New Testament doctrines of our " great salvation."

That devout and profound teacher of the Word, the late Dr. Adolph Saphir, used often to express his "grief and astonishment" at the prevalent neglect of the Old Testament. In his beautiful and helpful work, "Christ and the Scriptures," he says: "As a dictionary is necessary to explain the words of a new language, so the words and facts of the Gospels require the explanation of Moses and the prophets. You cannot read the New Testament without using the Old as a dictionary." This is a true testimony. " Scripture knowledge derived from the knowledge of Scripture is the best kind of knowledge." The Bible is its own interpreter.

One result of the recent fearful developments of grievous fundamental error concerning the Person and work of our Lord Jesus Christ, "Who is over all, God blessed for ever," is that it has called forth, to His praise and glory, precious testimonies to the Divine fulness, unity, and authority of the God-breathed Scriptures, that otherwise might not have appeared. Such a testimony is exampled in the following pages and other publications from the same pen.

The Old Testament has long been a special object of attack—and more particularly the Pentateuch. What a testimony, and that in an evangelical sense, to its historic verity—including all that relates to the description, construction, erection, and service of " the Tabernacle of Witness in the wilderness "— lies in the fact that, in His Road-to-Emmaus discourse, our risen Lord began His exposition of Himself " at Moses " ; " all the prophets " too, but *Moses first*—Moses, of whom He had testified, " Moses wrote of Me." Might we not add, " and in whom He Himself wrote "?

No wonder the hearts of those two disconsolate disciples burned within them while the Lord, book in hand, so to speak, walked and talked with them, expounding His own Scriptures, and all "concerning Himself." Can He, will He, so walk and talk with us to-day? He can, He will. Ask Him, my reader, as, Bible in hand, you scan closely these beautiful, clear, Scriptural "Outlines." Begin at the beginning, comparing Scripture with Scripture. Find your Emmaus-journey as in heart and mind you pass from East to West of the Divine dwelling. Look up into the face of the Antitype as you study the type; mark both the comparison and the contrast. Thus will an open Bible become to you an opened Bible indeed, Luke xxiv. 32, 45. Then rise up the same hour and go and tell others of Him who appeared to you "in the way."

"UNTO HIM THAT LOVETH US, AND LOOSED US FROM OUR SINS BY HIS BLOOD, AND HE MADE US TO BE A KINGDOM, TO BE PRIESTS UNTO HIS GOD AND FATHER; TO HIM BE THE GLORY AND THE DOMINION FOR EVER AND EVER. AMEN."

FRANK H. WHITE

The Tabernacle and Its Court

CONTENTS

The Kohathites upon their shoulders bare
The holy vessels covered with all care ;
The Gershonites receive an easier charge—
Two wagonsful of cords and curtains large ;
Merari's sons four ponderous wagons load
With boards and pillars of the House of God.

R. McCheyne

OUTLINE STUDIES OF THE TABERNACLE

———•••———

I

The Tabernacle

(1) The place where God *meets* the sinner, Exod. xxv. 22 ; xxix. 42, 43.

Now He meets us in Christ, 2 Cor. v. 19.

(2) The place where God *reveals* Himself to the sinner, Exod. xxix. 46.

Now He reveals Himself in Christ, John xiv. 7–9.

(3) The place where God *dwells* with sinners, Exod. xxv. 8 ; xxix. 45, 46.

Now He dwells with us in Christ, Matt. i. 23 ; John xiv. 23.

(4) The place where God *speaks* with the sinner, Exod. xxix. 42 ; Lev. i. 1.

Now He has spoken to us in Christ, Heb. i. 2 ; John viii. 43, 47 ; John i. 1.

(5) The place where God *accepts* the sinner, Lev. i. 4.
Now He accepts us in Christ, Eph. i. 6.

(6) The place where God *forgives* the sinner, Lev. iv.
20, 26, 31, 35 ; v. 10, 16, 18 ; vi. 7.
Now He forgives us in Christ, Eph. i. 7.

(7) The place where God *receives from* the sinner,
Exod. xxiii. 15 ; xxviii. 38.
Now He receives from us in Christ, Heb. xiii.
15.

The Encampment of BENJAMIN, EPHRAIM, and MANASSEH

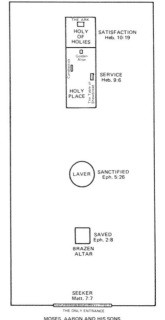

**Diagram of
Tabernacle
with Position
of Tribes**

The Encampment of SIMEON, REUBEN, and GAD

The Encampment of ASHER, DAN, and NAPHTALI

THE ARK
HOLY OF HOLIES — SATISFACTION Heb. 10:19
Golden Altar
Candlestick — SERVICE Heb. 9:6
HOLY PLACE — The Table of Shewbread

LAVER — SANCTIFIED Eph. 5:26

SAVED Eph. 2:8
BRAZEN ALTAR

SEEKER Matt. 7:7
THE ONLY ENTRANCE

MOSES, AARON AND HIS SONS
The Encampment of ZEBULUN, JUDAH, and ISSACHAR

II

Reasons for Studying the Tabernacle

Because—

(1) So many chapters * in the Bible are taken up with its description and ritual.

(2) God Himself thought so much of the importance of the type, as shown by the rending of the vail.

(3) It speaks to us of the Lord Jesus Christ, *e.g.*, Heb. x. 20.

(4) It was designed by the Holy Spirit, Heb. ix. 8.

(5) There is much of the New Testament which we could not understand without it, *e.g.*, the Epistle to the Hebrews.

(6) Its study is a sure antidote to the poison of unsound teaching—the so-called "New Theology" of various sorts—as to sin, atonement, the Person and character of the Lord Jesus Christ.

(7) It will make us proof against all doubts of the inspiration of Scripture, and all the attacks of so-called "Higher Criticism."

(8) Its teaching covers in type almost the whole range of New Testament truth.

---

* 13 in Exodus, 18 in Leviticus, 13 in Numbers, 2 in Deuteronomy, and 4 in Hebrews. These 50 chapters tell us of the construction, the ritual, the priesthood, the carrying of the Tabernacle, and the meaning of it all.

11

III

God's Dwelling Places

The Tabernacle typifies Christ and His Church as God's dwelling place now—in wilderness days, or journeying from place to place in the land.

The Temple typifies Christ and His Church in resurrection glory—no more journeyings, but established for ever—His kingdom having been set up.

(1) The Tabernacle, Exod. xxv. 8 ; xxix. 45, 46.

(2) The Temple, 2 Chron. vi. 1, 2.

(3) The Lord Jesus Christ—Antitype of the Tabernacle, "tabernacled among us," John i. 14 ; and of the Temple, John ii. 20, 21.

(4) The Church of God—
Individually and collectively, Eph. ii. 21, 22 ;
Now in humiliation as the Tabernacle ;
By-and-by in glory as the Temple, Eph. ii. 21, 22 ; 1 Pet. ii. 5.

(5) The future Tabernacle and Temple, Rev. xv. 5 ; xxi. 3.

(i.) PREPARATION FOR EACH

(1) Exod. xi. 2 ; xii. 35, 36; xv. 2 ; xxxv. 4–35 ; xxxvi. 1–7.

(2) 1 Chron. xxii. 3, 5, 14 ; xxix. ; 2 Chron. viii. 16 ;
    1 Kings v. 17, 18.

(3) Heb. x. 5 ; Hosea vi. 3 ; Luke ii. 31.

(4) Luke i. 17 ; Rom. ix. 23.

(5) Isa. ii. 2 ; Rev. xxi. 2, 3.

(ii.) THE PATTERN

(1) Exod. xxv. 9, 40 ; xxvi. 30 ; xxvii. 8 ; Acts vii.
    44.

(2) 1 Chron. xxviii. 11, 12, 19.

(3) Hebrews i. 3 ; Gen. v. 1.

(4) Col. iii. 10 ; 2 Cor. iii. 18 ; Rom. viii. 29 ; 1 Cor.
    xv. 49.

(iii.) THE CLOUD, TYPIFYING THE HOLY SPIRIT

(1) Exod. xiii. 21, 22 ; Exod. xl. 34–38.

(2) 1 Kings viii. 10, 11 ; 2 Chron. v. 13, 14.

(3) Matt. xvii. 5 ; Mark ix. 7 ; Acts i. 9.

(4) 1 Cor. x. 1, 2, with 1 Cor. xii. 13.

(5) Ezek. xliii. 1–5 ; Rev. xv. 5, 8.

(iv.) GOLD, TYPIFYING THE DIVINE (see Job xxii. 25, *marg.*)

(1) Exod. xxxv. 5, etc.

(2) 1 Chron. xxii. 14, 16 ; xxviii. 14–18 ; 2 Chron. iv.
    19–22.

(3) John i. 1.

(4) 2 Pet. i. 4 ; 1 Cor. iii. 12 ; Rev. iii. 18.

(5) Rev. xxi. 18, 22.

(v.) THE EXTERIOR—THAT SEEN BY MEN

(1) Badgers' skins, Exod. xxvi. 14—comparatively unattractive.

(2) Gold and precious stones, 2 Chron. iii. 6 ; " Exceeding magnifical," 1 Chron. xxii. 5.

(3) Humiliation, Isa. liii. 2, 3 ; in transfiguration and resurrection glory seen by His own disciples, Matt. xvii. 2 ; John i. 14 ; 2 Pet. i. 16, 17.

(4) Pilgrims and strangers now, 1 Pet. ii. 11 ; 2 Cor. iv. 7–10 ; vi. 4–10; 1 John iii. 1 ; by-and-by the glory manifested, Eph. ii. 21 ; 2 Thess. i. 10; Rom. viii. 18, 19; 1 John iii. 2.

(vi.) THE SPIRIT'S WORK

(1) Exod. xxxi. 3–5 ; xxxv. 31–33 ; Heb. ix. 8.

(2) 1 Chron. xxviii. 19, 20 . 2 Chron. ii. 12.

(3) Luke i. 35.

(4) Eph. ii. 22.

(vii.) WILLING OFFERERS

(1) Exod. xxv. 2 , xxxv. 5, 21, 22, 29.

(2) 1 Chron. xxix. 5, 6, 9, 14, 17.

(3) Psa. xl. 8.

(4) Psa. cx. 3.

IV

The Altar of Burnt-offering

An altar most holy —*marg.* holiness of holinesses

Directions given, Exod. xxvii. 1–8 ; carried out, chap. xxxviii. 1–7 ; Altar brought to Moses, chap. xxxix. 39 ; new directions for anointing and setting up, chap. xl. 6, 10 ; set up and used, chap. xl. 29.*

Shittim wood overlaid with " brass " (copper). "Brass," that which will endure the fire of God's holiness, taken to typify judgment.

Foursquare, 5 cubits † in length and breadth (about 7½ feet). Sides facing north, south, east, and west, all equal—alike to all the world.

3 cubits high, grating half-way, viz., 1½ cubits high. The grating was on a level with the height of the Mercy-seat and Table of Shewbread.

No steps were allowed, Exod. xx. 26, but probably there was an inclined ascent. "Aaron came down from offering," Lev. ix. 22.

Its covering of purple, see page 34.

---

* It will be noticed that there is in Exodus a five-fold mention of each of the holy vessels of the Tabernacle.

† The cubit probably 18 inches.

It was so large that all the " vessels " of the Holy
Places could have been contained in it.
" Within the one great sacrifice of the Lord
Jesus on the cross every other is compre-
hended."

Fire fell upon it at the consecration of the priests
in token of God's acceptance of the sacrifice,
Lev. ix. 24.

(i.) THE ALTAR'S FURTHER HISTORY

In connection with David, 1 Chron. xxi. 29.
Solomon, 2 Chron. i. 5, 6.
Ahaz, 2 Kings xvi. 14, 15.
Hezekiah, 2 Chron. xxix. 27–35.
For Chart of the Offerings, see page 20.

(ii.) THE EAST END OF THE ALTAR

(1) " The place of the ashes," Lev. i. 16.   Ashes
denoted acceptance of the offering, Psa. xx. 3,
marg.   The fire had said, " It is enough,"
Prov. xxx. 16.

A place " holy unto the Lord," Jer. xxxi. 40.

The standing-place of the priests at the com-
pletion of the Temple, 2 Chron. v. 12 ; and
the standing-place of the redeemed through
all eternity—the place of accepted sacrifice.

(2) The east, the way of God's glory, Ezek. xliii. 1,
2, 4.   God's smile is always on the finished

work of the Lord Jesus Christ, and on those who come to Him through the one precious way."

(iii.) A Tabernacle Interpretation of Psalm CIII. 12

" As far as the east " (the entrance of the Tabernacle where the sinner came in with sin upon him) "is from the west" (the Mercy-seat, the throne, the place of communion), "so far hath He removed our transgressions from us."

> No blood, no altar now,
>   The sacrifice is o'er ;
> No flame, no smoke ascends on high,
>   The lamb is slain no more :
> But richer blood has flowed from nobler veins,
> To purge the soul from guilt, and cleanse the reddest stains.

General View of the Tabernacle

V

The Blood

It is the blood that maketh an atonement for the soul, Lev. xvii. 11.

Without shedding of blood is no remission, Heb. ix. 22.

(1) Sprinkled on the Tabernacle and its vessels, Heb. ix. 20–22.

(2) Blood of burnt-offerings and peace-offerings sprinkled round about upon the altar, or " wrung out " at its side, Lev. i. 5, 15 ; iii. 2, 13 ; viii. 24.

(3) Blood of sin-offering for priest or congregation sprinkled before the Lord, *before the vail*, put on the horns of altar of incense ; the rest poured out at the bottom of the brazen altar, Lev. iv. 6, 7, 17, 18 ; viii. 15 ; ix. 9, 18.

(4) Blood of sin-offering for ruler or one of common people put on the horns of altar of burnt-offering ; the rest poured out at the bottom, Lev. iv. 25, 30, 34.

(5) Blood of trespass-offering sprinkled upon the side of the altar ; the rest " wrung out " at the bottom of the altar, Lev. v. 9.

(6) Blood of bullock and goat on the day of atonement sprinkled *on* the Mercy-seat, eastward

(*i.e.*, in front) ; sprinkled *before the Mercy-seat* seven times, Lev. xvi. 14. Sprinkled on the horns of the altar of incense seven times, Lev. xvi. 18, 19 ; Exod. xxx. 10.

(7) Blood of red heifer sprinkled seven times *before the Tabernacle*, Num. xix. 4.

(8) At the consecration of the priests, put on the tip of the high priest's right ear, thumb of his right hand, great toe of his right foot ; the same for the priests, Lev. viii. 23, 24, some of the blood from the altar sprinkled on Aaron, his garments, and his sons and their garments, verse 30.

(9) At the cleansing of the healed leper the same, Lev. xiv. 7, 14.

The blood was for—

Remission and purging, Heb. ix. 22.

Purification, Lev. viii. 15 ; Heb. ix. 23.

Atonement, Lev. xvi. 16 ; Exod. xxx. 10.

Sanctification and reconciliation, Lev. viii. 15, 30. Always and everywhere the blood. The blood betokens a life laid down ; " for the life of all flesh is the blood thereof," Lev. xvii. 11, 14. The blood in the Tabernacle was literal blood, the blood shed at Calvary was real blood ; but in most of the New Testament references it means a *life laid down* (as 1 John i. 7), rather than the actual blood itself.

VI.—A Chart of the Levitical Offerings *

THE OFFERING.	CONSISTED OF	GOD'S PART ON THE BRAZEN ALTAR.	PRIESTS' PORTION.	TYPICAL OF THE LORD JESUS.	REFERENCES.
Burnt-Offering.	Bullocks, goats, sheep, rams, lambs, turtle-doves, young pigeons.	All burned.	Skin.	In His life and death, perfectly accomplishing the will of God.	Leviticus i. ; Leviticus vi. 8–13; Ephesians ii. 1–6; Hebrews x. 7.
Meal-Offering.	Fine flour, green ears, frankincense, oil, salt.	A handful, part of oil, all frankincense, all priests' offering.	All remainder.	As Man, presenting to God an unblemished life.	Leviticus ii. ; Leviticus vi. 14–23; Hebrews vii. 26.
Peace-Offering.	Male and female of herd and flock, bullocks, lambs, goats.	All the fat	Heave-shoulder, and wave-breast.	By His death becoming our peace and the ground of communion.	Leviticus iii. ; Leviticus vii. 11–13; Romans v. 1; Colossians i. 20.
Sin-Offering.	Male and female of herd and flock, or turtle-doves, young pigeons, $\frac{1}{10}$ ephah of flour.	All the fat, blood at the bottom of altar (and on horns of incense altar).	Offering where blood was not taken into Tabernacle.	On the Cross made sin for us.	Leviticus iv. ; Leviticus vi. 24–30; 2 Corinthians v. 21.
Trespass-Offering.				By His sacrifice becoming answerable for sins and transgressions against God and man.	Leviticus v. ; Leviticus vi. 1–7; Leviticus vii. 1–7; Colossians ii. 13, 14; 1 Peter ii. 24.

* From Ada R. Habershon, *The Study of Types* (Grand Rapids: Kregel Publications, 1957).

† It is generally stated that the meal-offering does not include the Lord's death. It is true there is no mention of blood, but Lev. ii. 14 speaks of the "firstfruits" as a meal-offering. This is a type of His resurrection, Lev. xxiii. 10, 11; 1 Cor. xv. 23. It seems evident that there must have been some reference to His death earlier in the chapter. This is found in verse 6: they were to "part in pieces" the loaf or cake, a type of the broken bread, 1 Cor. xi. 23, 24. Also the word for cakes in verse 4 implies "pierced cakes" (*Newberry*), and the action of fire (baking, &c.) suggests judgment.

VII

Symbols of the Lord's Sufferings

Perfect through sufferings

(1) The vail rent (see page 36).

(2) The offerings slain (see page 19).

(3) The blood poured out, wrung out, sprinkled (see page 18).

(4) The rams' skins dyed red (see page 33).

(5) The meal - offering roast with fire, parted in pieces, pierced (see Chart of Offerings, foot-note, page 20).

(6) Things bruised, crushed or beaten,* Isa. liii. 5, 10.

Fine flour for shewbread, Lev. xxiv. 5.

Fine flour for meal-offering, Lev. ii. 1.

Corn beaten out, Lev. ii. 14.

Manna ground, Num. xi. 8 ; Isa. xxviii. 28.

Oil for the light, Exod. xxvii. 20.

---

* Some of these (*e.g.*, the oil, spices, etc.), typify also the Holy Spirit ; but He was only given after the Lord had suffered and had been glorified, John vii. 39.   Others probably speak of His people in union with Himself—as in the candlestick, cherubim, and rent vail—"crucified with Christ," Gal. ii. 20 ; "the fellowship of His sufferings," Phil. iii. 10.

Oil for the meal-offering, Exod. xxix. 40 ("Geth-
semane" means "oil-press").

Spices crushed.

Incense beaten small, Exod. xxx. 36.

Gold for candlestick, Exod. xxv. 31, 36; Num.
viii. 4.

Gold for cherubim and Mercy-seat, Exod. xxxvii.
7.

VIII
The Laver

Directions given, Exod. xxx. 18–21 ; directions carried out, chap. xxxviii. 8 ; brought to Moses, chap. xxxix. 39 ; directions for setting up and anointing, chap. xl. 7, 11 ; laver set up and used, chap. xl. 30–32.

Made of " brass," or copper, from the mirrors of the women, Exod. xxxviii. 8.

No measurements given—God's provision for cleansing is unlimited.

Typifies " the washing of water by the Word," Eph. v. 26.

The water with which it was filled at the first setting up of the Tabernacle at Sinai must have been the water from the smitten rock, which typifies the Holy Spirit, see John vii. 39. The Word was inspired by the Spirit, and must be applied in the power of the Spirit.

Was for the use of those who already belonged to the family of Aaron or the tribe of Levi ; and the cleansing at the laver is for those who are already God's children—it does not make them so, and does not typify regeneration ;

John xiii. repeats and explains the type. Verse 10, " He that is washed (regenerated, as in Titus iii. 5) needeth not, save to wash his feet " (the laver). The first for salvation, the second for communion.

It was for use after going, and when going, to the altar ; and before going in to worship in the Holy Place, in order to remove defilement from contact with the earth.

It is the provision for our need between the cross (the altar) and the glory (inside the vail), Eph. v. 27. " Whither the Forerunner is for us entered."

(i.) CLEANSING BY THE WORD

Psa. cxix. 9 ; John xv. 3 ; xvii. 17, 19 ; Eph. v. 26.
An instance. " Peter remembered the Word of the Lord," Luke xxii. 61, 62.

(ii.) THE WORD A MIRROR

In which we see—ourselves, James i. 23–25.
In which we see—Himself, 1 Cor. xiii. 12.

(iii.) GOD'S TWO-FOLD PROVISION FOR CLEANSING.

Represented by the altar and the laver—the blood and the water.
The altar, Eph. v. 25 ; the laver, Eph. v. 26.
Blood and water, Lev. xiv. 5–7 ; Heb. ix. 19 ; John xix. 34 ; 1 John v. 6, 8.

(iv.) CLEAN HANDS

(1) For acceptance, Psa. xxiv. 3, 4.

(2) For increased strength, Job xvii. 9.

(3) For drawing nigh, James iv. 8.

(4) For worship, Psa. xxvi. 6.

(5) For reward, 2 Sam. xxii. 21, 25.

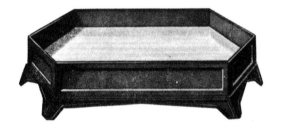

The Brazen Laver

IX

God's Seven-fold Provision for Defilement of Various Kinds

(1) The sin-offering.

   Sins of ignorance against any of the command-
      ments of the Lord, Lev. iv. 2, 13, 22, 27.

(2) The trespass-offering.

   Hearing false swearing, chap. v. 1.

   Touching certain unclean things, vers. 2, 3.

   Concerning an oath, ver. 4.

   Sins of ignorance in the holy things of the Lord,
      ver. 15.

   Breaking Eighth, Ninth, or Tenth Command-
      ment, Lev. vi. 2, 3.

(3) The day of atonement.

   The guilt of Aaron and his house and the con-
      gregation, Lev. xvi.

(4) The red heifer.

   Contact with death, Num. xix. (accidental or
      necessary).

(5) The cleansing of the leper.

   To remove all taint after leprosy had been healed,
      Lev. xiv

(6) The laver.

    Contact with earth, washing of hands or feet.

(7) The plate on the High Priest's mitre.

    Iniquity of their holy things, Exod. xxviii. 36–38.

The first four give different aspects of Christ's work on Calvary.

The fifth, His death and resurrection.

The sixth, application of His work by the Word.

The seventh, the present work of the High Priest.

The first five have to do with the brazen altar, and other parts of the Tabernacle.

The sixth with the laver.

The seventh with the High Priest's dress.

X

Fire and Water

To ascertain the typical meaning of details, the best way is to look up the word in the Concordance, and study it with the context. If searching into the meaning of such things as " fire " and " water," note their purpose and their work in order to determine their meaning, for it is not always the same.

(i.) FIRE —" OUR GOD IS A CONSUMING FIRE "

Fire speaks of the presence of God and the holiness of God ; and as different attributes are displayed by that presence, and His holiness operates in different ways and with varied purposes, so fire in Scripture bears different meanings.

(1) *Fire from heaven spoke of acceptance*

(1) On the altar of burnt-offering, Lev. ix. 24 ; 2 Sam. xxii. 9, 13 ; Psa. xx. 3 (*marg.*).
(2) On Abel's sacrifice (probably this was how God showed His acceptance), Gen. iv. 4 ; Heb. xi. 4.
(3) On Gideon's, Judges vi. 21.
(4) On Manoah's, Judges xiii. 19, 20.
(5) On David's, 1 Chron. xxi. 26.
(6) On Solomon's, 2 Chron. vii. 1, 3.
(7) On Elijah's, 1 Kings xviii. 24, 38.

(2) *Fire spoke of judgment*

(1) When it fell on Sodom, Gen. xix. 24.

(2) In Egypt, Exod. ix. 23, 24.

(3) On Nadab and Abihu, Lev. x. 2.

(4) In the camp, Num. xi. 1.

(5) At Korah's rebellion, Num. xvi. 35 ; xxvi. 10.

(6) On Azariah's messengers, 2 Kings i. 10–14.

(7) When it consumed the sin-offering outside the
camp, Lev. iv. 19.*

(3) *Judgment in the future*

(1) On Israel, Matt. iii. 11, 12.

(2) On His enemies at the Lord's coming in glory,
2 Thess. i. 8 ; Isa. x. 16, 17 ; Isa. lxvi. 15, 16.

(3) On the rebels after the millennium, Rev. xx. 9.

(4) Eternal judgment, Rev. xx. 10, 14, 15.

(4) *Testing and trial*

(1) During the life, 1 Pet. i. 7 ; Prov. xxv. 4.

(2) Israel in the future, Mal. iii. 2 ; Zech. xiii. 9 ; Isa.
iv. 4.

(3) At the judgment-seat of Christ testing believers'
works, 1 Cor. iii. 13, 15 ; with Num. xxxi. 23.

(5) *The Holy Spirit*

(1) The descent of the Holy Spirit was accompanied
with "tongues as of fire," Acts ii. 3.

---

* A different word is used for burning in Lev. i., where, in
reference to the altar of burnt-offering, it means ascending as
incense.

(2) Fire which gives light for guidance—as in pillar of fire; or testimony—as in candlestick, also speaks of the Holy Spirit.

(6) *The Word*

Jer. v. 14; xx. 9; xxiii. 29.

(ii.) WATER

(1) Where it is a question of cleansing by washing or sprinkling, the water means *the Word*, Eph. v. 26. See notes on laver.

(2) Water which gives life, refreshment, or fruitfulness, by drinking in or flowing out, typifies *the Holy Spirit*, John vii. 37, 39. See "rivers of water," "showers of blessing."

(3) Rain which destroys, as in the flood, or Matt. vii. 25, speaks of *judgment*.

(4) Water which threatens danger and death speaks of *death*, as in the crossing of the Red Sea and Jordan.

(5) "Water spilt on the ground" tells of *man's weakness*, 1 Sam. vii. 6; 2 Sam. xiv. 14; Psa. xxii. 14.

(6) Water in its turmoil and unrest is a simile of the *nations*, Rev. xvii. 15; Isa. lvii. 20.

In several passages the Word and the Spirit are linked together. "Born of water and of the Spirit" cannot be mere repetition; but the water is evidently the Word, as in 1 Pet. i. 23: "Born again . . . by the Word of God."

The Curtains and Coverings

Directions given, Exod. xxvi. 1–14; carried out, chap. xxxvi. 8–19; brought to Moses, chap. xxxix. 33, 34; commands to set them up and anoint them, chap. xl. 2, 9; carried out, chap. xl. 17–19.

(i.) THE EMBROIDERED CURTAINS—THE TABERNACLE ITSELF

Ten in number, each curtain 28 cubits long and 4 cubits wide; joined together in two sets of five; these sets being joined together by 50 taches of gold and 100 loops of blue. The taches were immediately above the vail that divided between the Holy Place and the Holiest of All, Exod. xxvi. 33.

Fine twined linen, and blue, and purple, and scarlet; and embroidered with cherubim. Typified the character and glories of the Lord Jesus Christ.

Fine twined linen—His spotless purity; linen representing, as in Rev. xix. 8, righteousness.

Blue—His heavenly character, John iii. 13.

Purple—The royalty of Christ. Purple chiefly refers to the Gentiles; only once or twice is it inclusive of Israel, Judges viii. 26; Jer. x. 9;

Ezek. xxvii. 7, 16 ; Acts xvi. 14 ; Esther i. 6 ;
viii. 15 ; Dan. v. 7, 16, 29 (*marg.*).

Scarlet—Christ's earthly glory. (Same word for
worm, Job xxv. 6 ; Psa. xxii. 6.) Specially
connected with Israel or Judah—the national
colour.

In Matthew's Gospel the Lord is represented as the
Son of David—the scarlet.

In Mark we see Him as the perfect Servant—the
fine twined linen.

In Luke He is the Son of Man—the One who will
wear the many crowns, Rev. xix. 12, 16—the
purple.

In John we see Him as the Son of God—the blue,
the heavenly colour.

The same colours were used for the vail, the hanging
for the door of the Tabernacle, and the gate
of the court.   There are no cherubim mentioned in the description of the last two.   All
three hangings were equal in area, viz., 100
square cubits ; the two in the Tabernacle were
10 cubits ; the gate of the court 20 × 5.

(ii.) THE GOATS' HAIR CURTAINS

Eleven in number, each curtain 30 cubits long (2
cubits longer than the Tabernacle), 4 cubits
wide.   Six curtains joined together in the
front, the sixth being doubled over the entrance, and five curtains at the back.   These

sets were coupled together by 50 taches of brass and 100 loops.

Goats were used in many of the offerings; but especially on the great day of atonement, when two goats were taken—one slain, and the other the scapegoat.

(iii.) RAMS' SKINS DYED RED

No dimensions given. Rams were also offered on many occasions, but the ram of consecration is specially mentioned. "Dyed red": this evidently spoke of suffering unto death.

(iv.) THE COVERING OF BADGERS' SKINS

No dimensions given. Kind of skin uncertain.

Probably denotes separation from evil, for everything was protected by them. See Heb. vii. 26; comp. Ezek. xvi. 10, "shod with badgers' skin."

The badgers' skins, which entirely hid the glories beneath, speak also of the humiliation of the Lord in His earthly life and ministry. (Contrast the outward glories of the Temple, see page 14.) Psa. xxii. 6; Isa. liii. 2, 3; Mark vi. 3; John i. 10; Phil. ii. 6, 7.

(v.) THE CURTAINS OF THE COURT

Fine linen. The whole Tabernacle was surrounded by that which spoke of the righteousness of God.

(vi.) THE COVERINGS OF THE HOLY VESSELS
(Num. iv. 5–15)

The Ark was covered with (1) the vail; (2) badgers'
skins; (3) cloth of *blue*.

The table of shewbread by (1) cloth of blue;
(2) cloth of *scarlet*; (3) badgers' skins.

The Candlestick and the golden Altar by (1) cloth
of *blue*; (2) badgers' skins.

The brazen Altar (1) cloth of *purple*; (2) badgers'
skins.

All, therefore, were covered with badgers' skins to
protect and to hide from the eyes of men.

The Ark alone had the *blue* on the outside; and
when the camp journeyed, when the children
of Israel crossed the Jordan, when the priests
carried it round the walls of Jericho, the blue
was visible. As we bear His name about
from place to place our testimony must always
be a heavenly one.

The Table of shewbread, which specially spoke of
provision for the twelve tribes of Israel, alone
had a *scarlet* covering.

The Altar, which most clearly typified " the sufferings of Christ," told in the *purple* covering of
" the glory that shall be revealed " in His
future kingdom.

XII

The Vail

Directions given, Exod. xxvi. 31–37 ; carried out, chap. xxxvi. 35, 36 ; brought to Moses, chap. xxxix. 34 ; directions for setting up, chap xl. 3 ; set up, chap. xl. 21.

Ten cubits square (about 15 feet) ; of blue, and purple, and scarlet, and fine-twined linen (see page 31) ; embroidered with cherubim (see page 57).

Divided between the Holy Place and the Holiest of All, Exod. xxvi. 33.

Designed by the Holy Spirit to teach a most important lesson. " The Holy Ghost this signifying, that the way into the Holiest of All was not yet made manifest, while as the first Tabernacle was yet standing," Heb. ix. 8.

Typified the incarnation of the Lord Jesus Christ. " The vail, that is to say, His flesh," Heb. x. 20. " Mere incarnation can do nothing for the sinner. We are saved by the death of Christ. The antitype of the unrent vail is seen at Bethlehem, at Nazareth, and all the life long of the Christ of God. The miracles of grace wrought during His ministry were like the swaying of the folds of that vail before men's eyes; and so were His words of grace from day to day, Luke iv. 22; John vii. 46: while Matt. xvi. 21 is as if, standing before the vail and pointing to it, He had said, That vail must be rent."

The vail was rent, "in the midst," Luke xxiii. 45; "from the top to the bottom," Matt. xxvii. 51; Mark xv. 38. Not from the bottom to the top, as though man had had anything to do with it, but "from the top to the bottom"; for it was the hand of God that thus made the type accurate. If it had remained unrent one minute after the Saviour had died, the type would have been incorrect. This shows the immense importance God attaches to His types.

Against these passages in the Gospels we might write, "The Holy Ghost this signifying, that the way into the Holiest of All *is now* made manifest."

It was called "the covering vail," Num. iv. 5:
(1) because it covered the Ark from sight when the Tabernacle was standing, Exod. xl. 3;
(2) because in journeying through the wilderness it was placed over the Ark, Num. iv. 5.

Thus none saw the gold of the Ark. The Lord's incarnation veiled His deity.

"Vailed in flesh the Godhead see."

(i.) THE VAIL—THE INCARNATION

John i. 14 ; 1 Tim. iii. 16 ; 1 John iv. 2, 3 ; 2 John 7.

(ii.) THE RENDING OF THE VAIL—HIS DEATH.

Heb. ii. 14 ; Rom. viii. 3 ; 2 Cor. v. 15, 16.

(iii.) WHY THE VAIL WAS RENT

To "bring us to God," 1 Pet. iii. 18.

To consecrate "a new and living way" of access to God, Heb. x. 20 ; ix. 8.

"To present (us) holy and unblameable and unreproveable in His sight," Col. i. 22.

To do "what the law could not do," Rom. viii. 2, 3.

(iv.) WITHIN THE VAIL—SINCE IT HAS BEEN RENT.

The High Priest has entered "by His own blood," Heb. ix. 12.

He now appears "in the presence of God for us," Heb. vii. 25 ; ix. 24.

Our "anchor" is fixed, Heb. vi. 19.

We ourselves may "come boldly" and "in full assurance of faith," Heb. iv. 16 ; x. 20, 22.

Our High Priest has entered as "the Forerunner," and we shall follow Him, Heb. vi. 20.

The rent vail not only made a way of access, but afforded unobstructed vision. Not only are we by faith permitted to approach, but by faith can gaze on that which was hidden before, Heb. ii. 9.

Exod. xxvi. 32, etc.   The vail was hung on "four pillars of shittim wood overlaid with gold ; their hooks gold, upon the four sockets of silver." *   A meaning suggested for these, " The four evangelists, human but inspired, reposing on redemption, holding up to view ' God manifest in the flesh.' "

---

* The hundred sockets of silver upon which the Tabernacle stood, and the hooks and fillets of the outer court, were made from the redemption money, Exod. xxxviii. 25-28.   Silver, therefore, typifies redemption.

XIII
The Altar of Incense

Directions given, Exod. xxx. 1–10 ; carried out, chap. xxxvii. 25–29 ; Altar brought to Moses, xxxix. 38 ; directions for setting up and anointing, chap. xl. 5, 9 ; directions carried out and incense burnt, vers. 16, 26, 27.

Shittim wood overlaid with gold ; 1 cubit square, 2 cubits high ; stood in the Holy Place, before the vail ; incense offered on it every morning and every evening, Exod. xxx. 7, 8.

No mention of it in Hebrews, because the vail has been rent, and we now offer spiritual incense at the Mercy-seat, Heb. iv. 16.

INCENSE

Ingredients :—Three sweet spices and frankincense in equal quantities, Exod. xxx. 34. The spices may be taken to typify the Spirit's work.

There were nine ingredients in the anointing oil and incense, Exod. xxx. 23, 34.

Nine chief spices in the garden, Song of Sol. iv. 13, 14.

Nine-fold cluster of the fruit of the Spirit,
Gal. v. 22, 23.

Nine gifts or operations of the Spirit, 1 Cor. xii.
8–10.

Nine-fold example of patience, 2 Cor. vi. 4, 5.

Nine virtues in 2 Pet. i. 5–7.

Incense might only be offered by the priests, *i.e.*, those
born into the family of Aaron. This explains
the sin of Uzziah, 2 Chron. xxvi. 18 ; com-
pare 2 Chron. xiii. 10, 11 ; Deut. xxxiii. 10 ;
1 Chron. vi. 49 ; ix. 30. None but those who
have been born again can offer incense to
God.

Strange incense might not be offered, Exod. xxx. 9.
Probably this was the sin of Nadab and
Abihu.

The most holy incense might only be used for God,
Exod. xxx. 37, 38.

Incense, like ointment, can be spoilt, Eccles x 1 ;
Isa. i. 13 ; and thus becomes an " abomination "
to God.

Incense typified :

(1) Christ Himself, " a sweet savour of Christ,"
2 Cor. ii. 14, 15.

(2) His Name, Song of Sol. i. 3.

(3) Prayer, because offered in His Name, Psa.
cxli. 2 ; Rev. v. 8 ; viii. 3 ; John xvi. 23, 26.

Other things are compared to ointment or spices,

and they may be as incense to God when "in His Name."

(4) Communion, Prov. xxvii. 9.

(5) Love, Song of Sol. i. 12 ; iv. 10 ; Matt. xxvi. 7 ; John xii. 3.

(6) Gifts, Phil. iv. 18.

At the golden Altar Uzziah was stricken with leprosy for his presumption, 2 Chron. xxvi. 18, 19. And "in the year that King Uzziah died," Isaiah there obtained cleansing and received his commission, Isa. vi. 6.

The time of the evening sacrifice (on the brazen Altar) and the time of the offering of incense (on the golden Altar) were often times of special crisis and answered prayer, Psa. cxli. 2.

Elijah, 1 Kings xviii. 29 ;

Ezra, Ezra ix 5 ;

Daniel, Dan. ix. 21 ;

Cornelius, Acts x. 2, 3, 30, with chap. iii. 1.

"The ninth hour." At the time the Lord died on the cross, the priest in the Temple must have been offering incense, and thus was probably standing in front of the vail when it was rent, Luke xxiii. 44 ; Matt. xxvii. 45, 46.

The *hour* of the Lord's death was foretold in the daily offering of the incense and the evening sacrifice ; the *day* was foretold in the Passover, and the *year* in Daniel's prophecy, Dan. ix. 25, 26.

When the High Priest entered the Holiest of All once a year, and stood in the presence of the Shekinah glory, he was shielded by a cloud of incense, " that he die not," Lev. xvi. 12, 13. " The Lord God is a Sun (the Shekinah glory) and Shield (the cloud of incense)," Psa. lxxxiv. 11.

The Altar of incense is not described in Exod. xxv. or xxvii., but in chap. xxx. " Now the priesthood has been instituted, there can be priestly worship " (*W. Lincoln*).

The offering of the incense by the High Priest in the Holiest of All was a beautiful type of our Lord's intercession, Heb. vii. 25 ; Heb. ix. 24 (see page 59).

XIV

The Table of Shewbread

Directions given, Exod. xxv. 23–30; carried out, chap. xxxvii. 10–16; brought to Moses, chap. xxxix. 36; new directions for setting it in order, etc., chap. xl. 4; carried out, vers. 22, 23.

2 cubits in length; 1 cubit in breadth; 1½ in height. Shittim wood overlaid with gold. 12 loaves of shewbread made of fine flour. Pure frankincense upon both rows, Lev. xxiv. 5–7. A token of an everlasting covenant, ver. 8. Fresh loaves placed on the Table every Sabbath, ver. 8. Those taken away eaten by the high priest and his sons, ver. 9. The frankincense all for God, as in the meat-offerings.

Two words for shewbread—Bread of "ordering," 1 Chron. ix. 32; xxiii. 29; xxviii. 16; 2 Chron. ii. 4; xiii. 11; xxix. 18; Neh. x. 33. Same word used for "row" in Lev. xxiv. 6, 7.

"Bread of faces," Exod. xxv. 30; xxxv. 13; xxxix. 36; Num. iv. 7.

Typifying Christ in the presence of God for us; the loaves were all the same size, though some of the tribes of Israel were much larger than others.

God First

There were three holy vessels in the Holy Place : the
golden Altar, the Lampstand, and the Table of
shewbread.   The primary aspect of each was
—something for God.

(1) The Candlestick was lighted "before the Lord,"
Exod. xl. 25.

(2) The bread on the Table was "before the Lord,"
ver. 23.

(3) The incense on the golden Altar was "before the
Lord," chap. xxx. 8.

The priests *saw* the light, *smelt* the incense, and
tasted the bread ; but each was for God first.

The Table of Shewbread Partly Covered

Types of Christ as Bread or Corn in Various Forms

(1) The bread of God from all eternity.

The manna, Psa. lxxviii. 24 ; cv. 40.

(2) The incarnation.

The manna, John vi. 33, 35, 50, 51.

(3) His perfect life.

The fine flour of the meal-offering, Lev. ii. 1.

(4) His death.

The "pierced" cakes, ver. 4* ; the cakes parted in pieces, ver. 6 ; the broken bread, 1 Cor. xi. 24.

(5) His resurrection.

The corn of wheat, John xii. 24 ; the corn of the land, Josh. v. 11, 12 ; the firstfruits, Lev. xxiii. 10, 11.

(6) His coming again.

The firstfruits, 1 Cor. xv. 23 ; the broken bread, 1 Cor. xi. 26.

(7) The food of His people.

The meal-offering, Lev. ii. 10 ; feast of unleavened bread, Lev. xxiii. 6 ; shewbread, Lev. xxiv. 9.

---

* See Chart of the Offerings, footnote, page 20.

(8) In the presence of God for us.
   The shewbread, Exod. xl. 23 ; the hidden **manna,**
      Rev. ii. 17.
(9) Typical incidents.
   Food in time of famine.
(10) A typical place.
   Bethlehem, the " house of bread."

The Golden Candlestick with Its Lamp and Vessels
(Uncovered)

XVI

The Candlestick or Lampstand

Directions given, Exod. xxv. 31–39 ; carried out, chap. xxxvii. 17–24 ; Candlestick brought to Moses, chap. xxxix. 37 ; directions given for setting up and lighting it, chap. xl. 4 ; carried out, vers. 24, 25.

Made of pure gold—one talent in weight, probably worth between £5,000 and £6,000, Exod. xxv. 39. Golden snuffers, chap. xxv. 38.

Seven branches—the centre shaft probably taller than the others. Comp. Heb. i. 9.

They gave light " over against " the candlestick, Exod. xxv. 37.

" A type of ministry on earth in the power of the Holy Spirit (the oil), having Christ for its source and subject." " The branches by themselves had no standing in the Sanctuary ; separated from the centre shaft, they ceased to be light-bearers." Comp. John xv. 4, 5.

The oil was " for the light." The Holy Spirit is given to us that we may shine for God.

The lamps were dressed by the High Priest every morning, Exod. xxx. 7. " In the process of trimming lamps there is a measure of offence ;

snuffs do not give forth a very dainty perfume :
. . . therefore before he trimmed the lamps the
priest kindled the incense " (*C. H. S.*).

They were lighted every evening, Exod. xxx. 8 ;
probably only burning during the night-time,
"from evening to morning." Comp. Exod.
xxvii. 20, 21 ; xxx. 7, 8 ; Lev. xxiv. 2, 3 ;
1 Sam. iii. 3 ; 2 Chron. xiii. 11.

The candlestick was carried into Babylon, Jer. lii. 19.

Used at Belshazzar's feast, when the handwriting on
the wall was "over against the candlestick,"
Dan. v. 2, 5. It was being used, not for God's
glory, but for the pleasure of the world ; and
thus God's judgment fell.

Christ walking in the midst of the seven golden
candlesticks, Rev. i. 12, 13, 20.

The Golden Candlestick with Its Lamps and Vessels
(Partly Covered)

XVII

Fruit and Light

The branches of the Lampstand were ornamented with almonds, knops, and flowers, symbolizing fruitfulness. These two similes of the work of the Spirit are often connected. Examples :—

Fruit	*Light*
(1) Lampstand.	
The ornaments on the branches.	The oil for the light.
(2) Joseph's dreams.	
The sheaves, Gen. xxxvii. 7.	Sun, moon, and stars, verse 9.
(3) Parable.	
The harvest in the parable of the tares.	"Then shall the righteous shine forth as the sun," Matt. xiii. 43.
(4) Command.	
"That ye bear much fruit," John xv. 8.	"Let your light so shine," Matt. v. 16.
(5) Epistles.	
Eph. v. 9.	Eph. v. 8, 9, 13 (R.V.).
Col. i. 6, 10.	Col. i. 12, 13.
Phil. i. 11.	Phil. ii. 15, 16.

XVIII

The Holy Spirit's Work in Reality and Symbol

(1) In the design of the Tabernacle, Heb. ix. 8.

(2) In the making of the Tabernacle, see page 14.

(3) In the anointing oil.

(4) In the oil for the light.

(5) In the oil for the meal-offering.

(6, 7) In the fruitfulness represented on the shafts of the lampstand, and the pomegranates on the priest's dress.

(8) In the spices of the incense.

(9) In the cloud over, and in the Holiest of All.

(10) In the Urim and Thummim, the "lights and perfections," in the breast-plate of the High Priest, Exod. xxviii. 30.

(11) In the water from the smitten rock used for the filling of the laver in the first instance—the Word inspired by the Spirit and applied by the Spirit.

XIX

The Ark

Directions given, Exod. xxv. 10–22 ; carried out, chap. xxxvii. 1–9 ; brought to Moses, chap. xxxix. 35 ; new directions for putting it in its place, chap. xl. 3 ; carried out, chap. xl. 20, 21.

2½ cubits in length, 1½ in breadth and height.

(i.) A TYPE OF THE LORD JESUS CHRIST

Made of shittim wood, Exod. xxxvii. 1.	The human nature of our Lord, Heb. ii. 14.
Overlaid with pure gold, Exod. xxxvii. 2.	His deity, John i. 1, 14.
The Mercy - seat pure gold, Exod. xxxvii. 6.	" Set forth to be a pro- pitiatory " (the same word), Rom. iii. 25.
The law placed in it,* Deut. x. 1–5.	" Thy law is within my heart," Psa. xl. 8.

---

* The law was God's covenant with Israel, laid up in the Ark, 2 Chron. vi. 11. Christ is the mediator of a better covenant— a covenant certain to be kept, for it is between God and Himself, Heb. ix. 15.

Going before to search out a rest, Num. x. 33.	" He goeth before them," John x. 4.
In the midst, Num. ii. 27.	Rev. i. 13 ; Matt. xviii. 20.
Going down into the river of death (Jordan), and thus enabling the people to go over dry-shod, Josh. iii.	Rom. vi. 3, 4. ; Col. iii. 1–4.
" When ye see the Ark . . . go after it," Josh. iii. 3.	" Looking unto Jesus," Heb. xii. 1, 2.
Bringing down strongholds (Jericho), Josh. vi.	2 Cor. x. 14 ; 1 John v. 5 ; Phil. iii. 21.
The place of confession, Josh. vii. 6.	Heb. iv. 16.
Taken by the foe, 1 Sam. iv. 11 ; Psa. lxxviii. 60, 61 (" the affliction of the Tabernacle," 1 Sam. ii. 32, *marg.*).	Mark xiv. 46 ; Acts. ii. 23.
Israel flies ; the Ark deserted, 1 Sam. iv. 10.	" They all forsook Him and fled," Mark xiv. 50.

Dagon falls, 1 Sam. v. 3, 4.

Enemies fall backward, John xviii. 6.

The strong man overcome, Luke xi. 22.

The way to get rid of idols, 1 John v. 21.

Seven months in the land of the Philistines ; death, 1 Sam. v. ; vi. 1.

A "savour of death unto death," 2 Cor. ii. 15, 16.

Three months in the house of Obed-edom, 2 Sam. vi. 10, 11.

A "savour of life unto life," 2 Cor. ii. 15, 16 ; John xiv. 23.

A triumphal entry, 1 Chron. xv.

Matt. xxi. 1 ; Luke xix. 29 ; John xii. 12–15.

Carried by Levites, 1 Chron. xv. 2.

"A chosen vessel to bear My Name," Acts ix. 15.

Brought into its place at last, 2 Chron. v. 7 ; xxxv. 3.

Heb. i. 3 ; Rev. xxi. 3.

David afraid at the sign of Divine majesty, 2 Sam. vi. 9.

Peter afraid at the sight of the Lord's power Luke v. 8, 9.

"We found it !" Psa. cxxxii. 6.

"We have found Him !" John i. 45.

Crossing the Cedron, 2 Sam. xv. 24.

"Over the brook Cedron," John xviii. 1.

None allowed to look inside it (the sin of the men of Bethshemesh, 1 Sam. vi. 19) or to touch it (the sin of Uzzah), 2 Sam. vi. 6, 7.

"No man knoweth the Son but the Father," Matt. xi. 27 ; Col. ii. 18.

Ministry before the Ark, 1 Chron. xvi. 37.

Eph. vi. 7 ; Col. iii. 24.

No more need to carry it, 1 Chron. xxiii. 26.

2 Tim. iv. 7, 8.

(ii.) THE HISTORY OF THE ARK'S JOURNEYINGS

At Sinai, Deut. x. 1 ; Exod. xl.

In the wilderness, Num. x. 33.

In Jordan, Josh. iii. ; iv.

Before Jericho, Josh. vi. 4–13.

At Gilgal, chap. iv. 19 ; ix. 6 ; x. 43

The valley of Achor, chap. vii. 6.

The vale of Shechem,* between Ebal and Gerizim, chap. viii. 33.

Shiloh, chap. xviii. 1 ; xix. 51 : Judges xxi. 19 ; 1 Sam. i. 3, 24.

The Battle at Ebenezer, 1 Sam. iv. 4.

Ashdod, Gath, and Ekron, 1 Sam. v. 1, 8, 10.

Bethshemesh, 1 Sam. v. 19.

---

* The scene in John iv. must have happened in the same place, ver. 5 ; Acts vii. 16.

Kirjath-jearim (Abinadab's house 20 years), 1 Sam.
    vii. 1, 2.
Fetched by David, 2 Sam. vi. 1–11 ; Psa. cxxxii. 6.
Obed-edom's house (3 months), 2 Sam. vi. 10–12.
Tent made for it by David, 2 Sam. vi. 17.
At Jerusalem in Zion, 2 Chron. i. 4 ; 2 Chron. v. 2
    (the Tabernacle being at Gibeon, 2 Chron. i. 3 ;
      1 Chron. xvi. 1, 39 ; xxi. 29).
In the Temple of Solomon, 2 Chron. v. 7–9.
Put back by Josiah, 2 Chron. xxxv. 3.
Seen by John in heaven, Rev. xi. 19.

**The Ark and
Mercy Seat
Partly Covered**

XX

The Contents of the Ark

The tables of stone, Deut. x. 1–5 ; Heb. ix. 4.

    (The covenant, 2 Chron. vi. 11.)

The book of the law in the side of the Ark, Deut. xxxi. 26.

The pot of manna, Exod. xvi. 33, 34 ; Heb. ix. 4.

Aaron's rod which budded, Heb. ix. 4.

Neither the manna nor Aaron's rod were in the Ark in the Temple (1 Kings viii. 9), probably because both were memorials of murmuring and rebellion, which will no more be remembered in the glory.

XXI
The Cherubim

Various interpretations of typical meaning, *e.g.*,
(1) the attributes of God; (2) His executive; (3)
emblems of the redeemed.

Embroidered on the curtains of the Tabernacle.

Embroidered on the vail, and therefore rent with it.

Of one piece with the Mercy-seat, Exod. xxv. 18–20;
    xxxvii. 7–9.

Looking toward one another, and toward the Mercy-
    seat, and therefore gazing on the blood.

These last facts seem to show that the cherubim
typify the redeemed; rent in the vail—crucified with
Christ, Gal. ii. 20; one with Him, John xvii. 21, 23;
fellowship with one another and with Himself, 1
John i. 3, 7; owing all to the blood, 1 John i. 7.

The Ark and
Mercy Seat

XXII

The Staves

Staves of Ark made, Exod. xxxvii. 5 ; put in for journeying, Num. iv. 6 ; withdrawn, 2 Chron. v. 9 ; the journey over.

Staves are an emblem of journeying.

Jacob's staff, Gen. xxxii. 10.

At the Passover, Exod. xii. 11.

Digging the wells, Num. xxi. 18.

Nothing for the journey save a staff, Mark vi. 8.

XXIII

Psalms xxvi and xxvii

Psalms xxvi. and xxvii. describe an approach toward the Holiest of All.

Psalm xxvi. 8 (*marg.*), delight in "the Tabernacle of Thine honour" ; ver. 6 the laver and the Altar.

Psalm xxvii. 1, the "light," the candlestick ; the "life," the table.

ver. 6, offering at the golden Altar.

ver. 4, the beauty of the Lord—the embroidered curtains and vail.

ver. 5, the secret of the Tabernacle—the Holiest of All.

XXIV

John's Gospel like the Tabernacle

The Word was made flesh, and tabernacled among us,
John i. 14.

Chapters i. to xii.—our Lord's public ministry on
earth in the outer court ; the first thing seen,
the Lamb for the Altar—" Behold the Lamb
of God, which taketh away the sin of the
world," chap i. 29 ; the last word to the out-
siders, chap. xii. 44–50.

Chapter xiii.—with His disciples alone—the laver
used and explained as preparation for ministry
in the Holy Place.

Chapters xiv. to xvi.—with them in the Holy Place,
teaching them about the Holy Spirit, the oil
for the light of the *candlestick*, also (chap. xv.)
the fruit-bearing represented on its branches ;
prayer in His name, the incense for the *golden
Altar* ; and His departure into the presence of
God, there to be the presence-bread on the
table of the shewbread.

Chapter xvii.—The High Priest alone in the Holiest
of All.

XXV

How the Tabernacle was Lighted

The outer court was lighted by the sun, with natural light, and could be seen by those outside.

The Holy Place by the candlestick, type of ministry of the Church.

The Holiest of All by the Shekinah glory of God's own presence.   Heaven itself will be like the Holiest of All.

" They need no candle (as in the Holy Place), neither light of the sun (as in the outer court) ; for the Lord giveth them light (as in the Holiest of All)," Rev. xxii. 5.

Even now we may have the "days of heaven upon the earth " (Deut. xi. 21), by dwelling in "the secret place of the Most High," Psa. xci. 1.

Index